Copyright 2021 by Miroslav Nikolić - All rig]

This document is geared towards providing exact and reliable information in regard to the topic and issue covered. The publication is sold on the idea that the publisher is not required to render an accounting, officially permitted, or otherwise, qualified services. If advice is necessary, legal or professional, a practiced individual in the profession should be ordered. From a Declaration of Principles which was accepted and approved equally by a Committee of the American Bar Association and a Committee of Publishers and Associations. In no way is it legal to reproduce, duplicate, or transmit any part of this document by either electronic means or in printed format. Recording of this publication is strictly prohibited and any storage of this document is not allowed unless with written permission from the publisher. All rights reserved. The information provided herein is stated to be truthful and consistent, in that any liability, in terms of inattention or otherwise, by any usage or abuse of any policies, processes, or Instructions: contained within is the solitary and utter responsibility of the recipient reader. Under no circumstances will any legal responsibility or blame be held against the publisher for any reparation, damages, or monetary loss due to the information herein, either directly or indirectly. By continuing with this book, readers agree that the author is under no circumstances responsible for any losses, indirect or direct, that are incurred as a result of the information presented in this document, including, but not limited to inaccuracies, omissions and errors. Respective authors own all copyrights not held by the publisher. The information herein is offered for informational purposes solely and is universal as so. The presentation of the information is without a contract or any type of guarantee assurance. The information herein is offered for informational purposes solely and is universal as so. The presentation of the information is without contract or any type of guarantee assurance. Readers acknowledge that the author is not engaging in the rendering of legal, financial, medical or professional advice. Please consult a licensed professional before attempting any techniques outlined in this book.

To all, who are in love with food, just like I am.

Table of Content

Table of Content 3

INTRODUCTION 7

Flashback 8

THE FOOD 13

A Day in Croatia 13

Essential Ingredients 15

Fruits and Vegetables...18

Seafood 20

Meat...23

Dairy Products, Pastries and Desserts.......................25

Drinks and Beverages 28

BREAKFAST RECIPES 31

Asparagus Frittata..32

Ham in Bread (Sunka U Kruhu)................................34

Breakfast Casserole with Ham and Bacon................36

Mushroom Pancakes...38

Mini Frittata with Quinoa 41

Ham and Cheese Bread (Prisnats) 43

Scrambled Eggs with Truffles....................................45

Sour Cherry Strudel 47

Eggplant with Marinated Feta Cheese 49

Stuffed Artichokes (punjeni artichoke) 51

Pumpkin Strudel (Bučnica) 53

Croatian Pršut and Škripavac 55

Lemon Oregano Bruschetta 57

SOUPS AND STEWS 59

Brown Roux (Prežgana) Soup..60

Croatian Zagorje Potato Soup..62

Mushroom Soup with Buckwheat 64

Leek Soup 66

Pasta and Bean Stew (Pasta Fazol)....................................68

Barley and Bean Stew..70

Bean and Sausage Stew 72

Rabbit Stew...74

Beef and Horse Stew (Cobanac) 76

Lamb Stew with Green Peas 78

Butternut Squash Stew..80

MAIN DISHES RECIPES...82

Black Risotto...83

Baked Strukli 85

Fried Squid Rings (Prženi Lignji)......................................87

Fuzi 89

Grilled Octopus (Hobotnica Na Zaru) 91

Grilled Sardines with Swiss Chard and Potatoes 93

Octopus Peka 95

Ham with Chestnuts 97

Chicken Paprika with Sour Cream 99

Grilled Chicken 101

Stuffed Bell Peppers 103

Shrimp Risotto 105

Croatian Mussels (Dagnje na Buzaru) 107

Croatian Buzara Shrimps 109

Swiss Chard and Potatoes 111

SALAD RECIPES 113

Tomato and Onion Vinegar Salad 114

Mixed Salad 116

Cabbage with Yoghurt Dressing 118

French Beans Salad 120

Octopus Salad (Salata od Hobotnice) 122

Fresh Cucumber Salad 124

Simple Bean Salad 126

French Salad (Francuska Salata) 128

DESSERT RECIPES 130

Paprenjaci (Gingerbread Cookies) 131

Fritule 133

Šnenokle 135

Black Cherry Cake 137

Prspajle (Fried Pastry) 139

Plum Jam Biscuits 141

Blackberry Pie 143

Coffee Crème Caramel...145

INTRODUCTION

In the northeastern part of the Balkan Peninsula, there is a small, crescent-shaped country known for its diversity. Despite its small size, it is rich in culture, customs, diversity, landscape, and history, all of which are expressed through its people, land, language, education, art, and, most notably, food. This is Croatia. Croatian cuisine is considered to be among the greatest in the world. You may try it at home with the collection of recipes in this book!

Croatia is surrounded by multiple countries, namely Slovenia, Hungary, Serbia, Montenegro and Bosnia and Herzegovina. Currently, three traditional regions comprise its crescent land: Slavonia, Istria, and Dalmatia. Slavonia is located in the country's upper arm, between the rivers Sava on the south and rivers Drava and Danube on the north and east. Istria is located on the Istrian Peninsula on the northern Adriatic coast, with the northern portion of the Istrian Peninsula belonging to the Republic of Slovenia and the northern and central portions belonging to Croatia. Finally, Dalmatia is where the land meets the sea. It is made up of coastal strips as well as several islands and islets scattered over the Adriatic Sea.

Historically, some countries and dynasties, such as the Ottoman empire and the Habsburgs, occupied certain sections of Croatia. Croatia has also been a part of Yugoslavia for several decades. All of this contributed to its long, winding history and added flavor to its national dishes, developing its great gastronomic traditions.

To truly develop a taste for a country's cuisine, one must first understand its culture, heritage, local produce, spices used, and influences from other cultures that contributed to the formation of this beautiful country. This is why it's important to start this cookbook with a quick flashback to the past.

Flashback

Complex, varied and regional. These are the dominant words that one will find after a day of surfing through the internet, trying to find descriptions of Croatian cuisine. Like any other country that is historically, culturally, and geographically diverse, Croatia's cuisine cannot be linked with only one flavor and categorized to a single type. Traditional Croatian food is a collection of a wide range of dishes that have been developed, improved, and passed on through time from one generation to another.

Croatia's continental region has been heavily impacted by surrounding and nearby cultures such as Austria, Hungary and Turkey. As a result, its recipes are generally meat and vegetable-based, with thick and spicy sauces made of black pepper, paprika, or garlic that provide rich flavor to every dish.

Two of the most recommended dishes of mainland Croatia are Cobanac and Kotlovina. Cobanac has been dubbed as a must-try for all meat lovers. It is a type of stew and is made up of various forms of meat, such as beef, pork, or lamb, vegetables, onions, and a delicious combination of sweet and fiery red peppers. The stew's richness and softness are the results of hours of preparation and cooking. Kotlovina, on the other hand, is also considered a deserving representative of the mainlander's cuisine.

Similar to Cobanac, Kotlovina can also be considered as a type of stew. It can be prepared by any type of meat, but the locals prefer pork. In the juice of fried meat and white wine, along with some herbs and spices, vegetables such as onions, peppers, potatoes are cooked. Once the sauce has reached the desired texture and the veggies are cooked, the marinated fried meat is added to the dish. Serving this stew with bread and wine completes the experience for mainlanders.

Aside from the mainland, Croatia's coastal region serves mostly Mediterranean-influenced dishes that emphasize the use of olive oil, rosemary, basil, and other fresh herbs and spices to add a twist and highly exquisite taste to its seafood-based cuisine. It keeps the traditional coastal cuisine light, nutritious, and unique.

Apart from its intact nature and white sand-studded sea coasts, the Croatian coastal cuisine is known for Peka and Pasticada. Peka is considered a versatile dish as it can include either seafood or meat. Due to its proximity to the sea, the seafood version is mainly served on Dalmatian islands. It starts with the octopus or other types of seafood in a round and thick baking pan that is mixed with potatoes and other vegetables by choice. The pan is then covered with a bell-shaped metal lid and is placed on burning wood. All sides of the pan, including its lid, must be covered with charcoal and embers to make sure all sides of the dish are cooked to perfection. This process takes hours as the dish requires slow cooking.

On the other hand, Pasticada represents the festive occasions of Dalmatia. This beef stew is one of the region's oldest recipes and takes a little time to cook. After marinating overnight, the marinated beef is cooked in its own juice for several hours to ensure tenderness. Once this is accomplished, figs, tomato puree, prunes, and Prosek, a form of sweet wine, are added.

These add flavor to the meat and leave a wonderful, long-lasting scent. Usually, the locals eat this dish along with some pasta or gnocchi.

Croatian cuisine is unquestionably the "cuisine of the regions" due to the country's varied offerings and flavors that test anyone's taste buds. However, as the next pages will show, Croatian cuisine has much more to offer.

THE FOOD

A Day in Croatia

Croatia's changes, like those of any other country that is constantly evolving, are visible and even extend to its tables. Its residents constantly balance and adapt their work hours, eating habits, leisure time, and culinary knowledge to the time and space. Despite all of the changes, Croatia's historic dining ritual is still practiced in the majority of homes.

A usual early-morning meal, considered as breakfast in Croatia, consists of hot bread rolls or bread from the local bakery, with plum jam and butter or slices of salami and cheese. Some people also prefer polenta or different dairy products. Breakfast is always paired with a cup of Turkish-style coffee.

After a few hours of working, Croatians take a break at 10 or 11 in the morning for Gablec. Gablec means a snack break, which is a very important and much-cherished custom. The most frequent dishes served during this time include beans stew with sausage or other soups and stews, Sarma, boiled veal with tomato sauce, mashed potatoes, and tripes.

In general, Croatians consider lunch to be their main meal. It starts with a tasty soup. The main course is then served, which could be meat or fish, but it is rarely a vegetarian dish. Vegetables, salads, or potatoes could be served as sides to meat or fish. Last but not least, a delicious homemade dessert usually follows the main course.

Dinner is heavily influenced by lunch, particularly the amount of food ingested. Some people prefer not to eat dinner, while others take a light meal to satiate their hunger. Most of the time, their dinner consists of cheese, grilled sardines, or other meaty goods served with bread.

Essential Ingredients

Obtaining the real flavor of Croatian cuisine begins with picking out quality, fresh and natural produce. The dish itself cannot be better than the produce used for creating it. Below are essentials ingredients that developed the identity of Croatian cuisine and characterized the taste of its dishes.

- **Vegeta.** It is a seasoning mix made out of different types of vegetables, such as celery, onion, garlic, parsley, parsnip, carrots and other vegetables and herbs. It can be in the form of a dry or fresh mixture and is used to season meat, soups and stews, gravies, sauces, risottos, pasta and other types of dishes – locals use it for almost every dish.
- **Olive Oil.** Cold press Olive oil is considered a must have cooking ingredient, as it is a base of many Croatian dishes. Due to the

Mediterranean climate, olive trees grow fantastically in Dalmatia. Most households in Dalmatia are therefore able to produce their own olive oil either for personal use or for resale.

- **Paprika.** It is mainly used by mainlanders, especially in the region of Slavonia. It is popularly used in sauces, gravies and stews, such as Paprikas and Gulyas. It is available in mild, smoked and spicy versions.

- **Potatoes.** Due to its versatility, potato is a very popular ingredient across all areas of Croatia. It is present in salads, included in Croatian Peka, fried, mashed, used for gnocchi, dumplings, and many other Croatia's signature dishes.

- **Ajvar.** It is a blend of eggplant and red bell peppers, along with herbs and spices. Ajvar is available in spicy and mild variations and is used as a spread over pita or bread, but most frequently, it is served with grilled meat.

- **Plum Jam.** It is a sweet, thick, sticky and absolutely delicious Croatian spread. It is made from local plums and is popularly used in baked goodies, such as pies and cakes, served for breakfasts or as a dessert.

- **Garlic.** Garlic is considered a must in most Croatian recipes as its strong flavor uplifts the taste of the soups, sauces, stews, meat or fish rubs, salads, and homemade food products, such as sausages.

- **Cabbage.** Cabbage could be eaten raw, in the form of a salad, pickled, or cooked. It is usually served in dressing or as a side dish for grilled meat. It can also be used in stews and soups or meat and cabbage rolls.

Croatian cuisine is constantly evolving, with new ingredients being added on a regular basis. Despite this, the aforementioned ingredients and dishes remain a basis of Croatian cuisine, serving as the anchor of many Croatian recipes that have survived throughout the years and will definitely keep their place in Croatian kitchens also in the future.

Fruits and Vegetables

Dalmatia, Istria, and the Croatian coast in rocky areas are known producers of wild asparagus, which is considered a delicacy in these areas. Its bitter and spicy taste is ideal for frittata, soups, pasta, and salads.

Istria is also recognized for its abundance of both white and black truffles. The distinctive and peculiar aroma of these gourmet mushrooms distinguished it and established it as one of the world's most prestigious truffles. These are used in pasta, risotto, omelets, meat dishes, and Motovun u Magli, an Istrian sweet treat.

Because the majority of Croatia has a Mediterranean climate, herbs grow well. Wild sage, for example, is produced mainly in Kornati Islands. Wild sage is known to contain essential oils with medicinal effects. Though it has a bitter taste, it is still used for oil and tea production due to its benefits. Furthermore, along the coastline, you can find a lot of rosemary and thyme bushes, different types of basil, bay leaf trees and all other Mediterranean herbs.

Like the herbs, olive trees grow well in the Mediterranean climate. Croatian olive oil is known to be of excellent quality and is widely exported to other members of the European Union as well as around the world. The olive trees grow well in the Istrian and Dalmatian areas, but the taste varies: some types of olive oil are stronger, with a taste of bitterness, and some have a milder taste.

In the southern part of Croatia, there is an area called Neretva. Its fertile soil is perfect for breeding fruits like the luscious Neretvanska Mandarina. This citrus fruit is a perfect source of vitamin C and is used to prepare juices, desserts, cakes, and other refreshing beverages. Among other popular types of fruit that grow in Croatia are plums, figs, peaches and watermelons.

Last but not least: grapes, which are usually purposed to become wine. The Istrian Malvasia or Istarska Malvazija, a type of white grapes, is popular for its high-yield, sweet and juicy taste. It is widely used in the production of a quality white, dry wine that holds the same name and is very popular throughout Croatia.

Seafood

Croatia has a never-ending coastline, with more than 1246 islands, 66 of which are inhabited. No wonder that seafood is extremely popular among the locals, as well as thousands of tourists that visit Croatian islands every year. Here are some popular examples of local seafood options.

- **Oysters**. Malis Ston's oysters are not only famous for their freshness but also for their aphrodisiac effect. It's a one-of-a-kind salty taste that makes it best consumed directly from the sea, paired with lemon or lime. It can also be served in soups, pasta, or deep-fried.
- **Mussels**. Mussels' production is widespread along the Adriatic coast, which is the reason why mussels are highly available in many restaurants and local stores along the coast. It is best cooked with garlic, wine, and tomatoes and served with bread or toast.
- **Sardines.** Mediterranean sardines are much larger than the ones found in other coastal countries. These are popular, especially to

those who reside along the coast. Locals highly encourage trying grilled sardines with grilled potatoes or tomatoes on the side.

- **Tuna**. The inclusion of the Bluefin tuna in the Croatian menu is a growing trend over the years. New recipes are introduced mainly by hotels and restaurants. They are even used as substitutes for pork and beef for their nutritional value.
- **Crabs and prawns**. Shellfish are extremely popular among the locals, as well as tourists. They are usually grilled, incorporated into a risotto, or cooked with white wine and garlic.
- **Noah's Ark**. Although these shellfish are nearly extinct, Croatians are still fond of these shells for their chewy, flavorsome taste and texture. Locals eat them raw, while some like them dipped in Buzara sauce or mixed with other shellfish or pasta.
- **Jellyfish**. Octopus, squids and cuttlefish are very popular. They are usually grilled or added to a risotto. Especially known is the black risotto, made out of cuttlefish. The black ink of the cuttlefish is added to make the risotto completely black. The octopus, however, is well known in the form of a simple salad with garlic, parsley and some mild seasoning.
- **Hake and sea bream** are among the popular white fish. Usually, locals prepare it on the grill, seasoned white fresh thyme, rosemary, garlic and pieces of lemon. As a side, mashed potatoes with chard are served.

Note that locals never overseason or overcook their seafood. Seafood is known for its fresh and mild taste, so it has to be left as natural as possible. You have to take precaution while cooking it: overcooked seafood might be mussy, chewy, or dried out.

Meat

Meat is especially popular in the Croatian mainland. Apart from its shore, which is noted for its seafood due to its abundance, the mainland, particularly Slavonia, is recognized for its meaty cuisine, such as stews, goulash, and grilled meat.

The following types of meat are popular in Croatia.

- **Pork**. The oldest breed of pig in Croatia, Turopoljska svinja, is highly regarded because of its succulent, juicy, and pinkish meat. It is best served as Samobor pork chops, Arambasi, or Sunka u kruhu.
- **Lamb**. The three major suppliers of lamb meat in Croatia are islands Cres, Pag, and Lika. Lamb meat is highly appreciated for its flavorful aroma and taste. It can be baked, spit-roasted, grilled, or breaded.
- **Turkey**. Zagorje's turkey meat is considered the best in all of Croatia. Zagorje is located in the northern part of Croatia, bordering on Slovenia. Its turkey is known to be tender and juicy. Also, it is very savory as they only fed their turkeys with organic

corn and grains. It is best roasted alongside Mlinci - a type of sheet pasta made with water, eggs, flour and a sprinkle of olive oil.
- **Beef.** Beef from islands Cres and Pag is considered the best in Croatia since it is fed on fresh grass. They are suited for pasticada, cevapi, and Sarma.
- **Chicken.** Like that of other countries, the breeding of chicken and usage of its meat is also widespread in Croatia. It is commonly used as a substitute for other meats because it is highly available in the market and is easier to cook. Beat Croatian chicken recipes are paprikas, Mediterranean chicken (Dalmatian style), and Croatian grilled chicken.

Dairy Products, Pastries and Desserts

Croatia, like other Balkan Countries, is known for its delicious cheese and desserts. Pag cheese is a popular type among the locals and tourists. It is a type of cheese that gave its name to the Island of Pag. It was specially produced from sheep's milk which is naturally salty after a day of grazing on salt-rich pastures due to its closeness to the sea. In addition, Croatian markets are rich in cottage cheese. Local farms produce cottage cheese with cow's milk solely. This type of cheese is most popular in Croatia's capital city, Zagreb and Zagorje area, as it became a traditional breakfast to their inhabitants.

Croatians are also great dessert makers. Among their most popular treats are Fritule. They taste similar to donuts and are traditionally made on days of fasting and on holidays and celebration days, such as Christmas. Due to its popularity, bakers sell these treats nowadays along the streets of Croatia. Usually, they are rolled in sugar while still warm. Various syrups also became a popular garnish for this dessert, so local bakers offer various toppings and coatings to choose from. They are certainly a must-try.

Another dessert you shouldn't miss out on is Salenjaci. It is a layered pastry filled with plum or apricot jam. It is sprinkled with sugar while still warm and is best served for early-morning meals or as a snack. Bajadera is also considered a traditional dessert in Croatia. It is a layered nougat with walnuts, almonds, or hazelnuts.

Furthermore, Rozata is a popular summer treat and is often served to foreign visitors. It is mainly made out of milk, sugar, eggs, and Rozulin - a rose liqueur. It resembles Creme Brule.

Last but not least, Cremeschnitte. Cremeschnitte is Samobor's pride and original dessert. It is a cake with a layer of cream and custard sandwiched between crispy filo pastries and is sprinkled with powdered sugar.

Drinks and Beverages

Like many other people around the world, Croatians are fond of coffee. Locals, sipping their choice of blend is a common sight on almost every street in every town at any time of the day because drinking coffee is regarded as a social event in Croatia. There are a number of coffee shops in Croatia. Some are freestanding, while others are attached to pastry shops or restaurants. In an average Croatian home, coffee is still cooked in Turkish style. The coffee is finely ground, mixed with water, and cooked on the stovetop in a handmade copper pot before being poured into a small cup. The fine coffee grounds settle to the bottom of the cup, leaving you with a delicious cup of coffee.

Among the alcoholic beverages, the most known is Pelinkovac. It is Croatia's oldest and most famous herbal liqueur, which is made from various herbs, along with its main ingredient, wormwood. It is believed to be an effective alternative medicine for stomach conditions and even improves digestion.

In addition, Croatia will never disappoint wine lovers as its history of wine production dates back thousands of years ago which only proves that its people already mastered this craft. They offer a wide range of wines, including white wine, red wine, and their pride, rose wine.

***

Above are just a few pieces of the Croatian cuisine's core that strengthen it and it links to the people of Croatia. More than its landscapes, seacoast, and history, Croatia's cuisine encompasses a wider range of food and recipes in terms of variety. Through this book, a trip to Croatia's finest regions is no longer necessary because a taste of authentic Croatian recipes lies in the next chapters.

BREAKFAST RECIPES

ASPARAGUS FRITTATA

Do you love asparagus? Then this recipe is for you. It's a great way of incorporating the veggie in your diet while making sure everyone enjoys breakfast.

| Prep time: 15 min | Cook time: 20 min | Servings: 4 |

Ingredients

- 2 tbsp unsalted butter
- ½ cup shallot, sliced
- 1 lb. asparagus, cut into 1-inch pieces
- 6 eggs, beaten
- ¾ cup ricotta cheese
- ½ tbsp salt
- 1 tbsp fresh chives, minced
- ¼ tbsp dried tarragon
- 1 cup Swiss cheese, shredded

Instructions

- Melt butter in a pan over medium heat.
- Sauté the shallots in butter for about 3 minutes.
- Stir the asparagus into the pan and cook for 3 minutes.
- Meanwhile in a bowl whisk the eggs, ricotta cheese, salt, chives, and tarragon.
- Pour the egg mixture over the asparagus and allow it to cook for about 4 minutes.
- Preheat the oven broiler.
- Sprinkle the eggs with Swiss cheese and place the frittata in the oven.
- Broil the frittata for 8 minutes.
- Slide the frittata onto a plate and slice.
- Serve and enjoy.

Nutrition-Per Serving: Calories: 465Kcal, Total Fat: 34g, Total Carbs: 11g, Protein: 31g

HAM IN BREAD (SUNKA U KRUHU)

The homemade dough is stuffed with ham to make a mix of wonderful savory flavors. Prepare this breakfast bread for your family and they will keep asking for more.

| Prep time: 1 h | Cook time: 1 h | Servings: 10 |

Ingredients

- 6 cup all-purpose flour
- ⅛ cup dried yeast
- 2 tbsp salt
- 1 tbsp sugar
- 1 ¾ cup warm milk
- ½ cup oil
- 3 lb. baked ham
- 1 egg, beaten

Instructions

- In a mixing bowl mix flour, yeast, salt and sugar until well combined.
- Stir ½ of the milk into the flour mixture and let the mixture stand for 10 minutes.
- Add oil and the remaining milk to the flour mixture and knead to smooth dough.
- Flour the kneaded dough on all sides and leave it covered for 45 minutes.
- Roll out the dough on a floured surface into a 2-inch rectangle.
- Coat the ham with the egg and place it on the rolled-out dough.
- Wrap the ham with the dough and place it on a baking sheet with the seam side down.
- Poke the dough with a fork and coat it with the remaining egg wash.
- Bake the bread in a preheated oven at 350°F for 20 minutes.
- Cover the bread with aluminum foil and bake for an additional 35 minutes.
- Place the bread on a cooling rack and cool for 10 minutes.
- Slice the bread and serve.

Nutrition-Per Serving: Calories: 552Kcal, Total Fat: 18g, Total Carbs: 62g, Protein: 34g

BREAKFAST CASSEROLE WITH HAM AND BACON

Shake up your breakfast routine with this breakfast casserole. It is easily put together and everyone, including your kids, will love it.

| Prep time: 10 min | Cook time: 45 min | Servings: 4 |

Ingredients

- 1 cup milk
- 6 cups cubed bread
- 4 oz bacon strips, sliced
- 4 scallions, chopped
- 8 oz ham, sliced
- 1 tbsp ground thyme
- Salt and black pepper to taste

- *1 tbsp butter*
- *4 eggs, beaten*

Instructions

- Preheat the oven to 375°F.
- Pour the milk into a medium-sized bowl and soak the bread for 10 minutes.
- Fry the bacon in a skillet over medium heat for approx. 3 minutes.
- Stir in the white parts of the scallions, ham, thyme, salt, and pepper to the bacon then cook for 5 minutes.
- Stir butter into the scallion mixture then remove it from heat.
- Stir in the eggs and remaining scallions to the bread mixture.
- Stir the egg mixture into the bacon mixture and transfer the mixture into a casserole dish.
- Bake the breakfast casserole for about 35 minutes.
- Serve and enjoy.

Nutrition-Per Serving: Calories: 422Kcal, Total Fat: 23g, Total Carbs: 26g, Protein: 25g

MUSHROOM PANCAKES

These pancakes are a super cheap way of preparing a healthy breakfast for your family. Bring the wonderful Croatian taste right into your kitchen with these pancakes.

| Prep time: 20 min | Cook time: 1h 15 min | Servings: 4 |

Ingredients

For the pancakes

- 2 eggs
- ⅔ cup milk
- ¼ cup soda water
- ¼ tbsp salt
- 1 cup all-purpose flour
- 2 tbsp butter

For the mushroom filling

- 3 ¼ tbsp butter
- 2 onions, chopped
- 1 ¼ cup mushroom, chopped
- Salt and black pepper to taste
- ¼ tbsp nutmeg
- 1 minced garlic clove
- ¼ cup beef stock
- ¾ cup sour cream
- 1 ½ tbsp chopped parsley
- 1 egg yolk

Instructions

- Whisk the eggs, milk, soda water, and salt in a bowl.
- Add flour gradually to the egg mixture until most of the lumps disappear.
- Heat ½ tablespoon of butter in a pan over medium heat.
- Add ¼ of the batter to the pan and swirl around to an even layer.
- Cook the pancake for 6 minutes, flipping it halfway through cooking. Repeat the process for all the pancakes. Set aside.
- Melt butter in a saucepan over medium heat and sauté the onions for 3 minutes.
- Stir in the mushrooms, salt, pepper, nutmeg, and garlic to the onions and cook for 3 minutes.
- Add the beef stock to the mushrooms and cook until most of the stock evaporates.
- Set the mushroom aside to cool.
- In a bowl, mix the sour cream, parsley, and egg yolk.
- Stir the sour cream mixture into the mushrooms.

- Scoop ¼ of the mushroom mixture onto each pancake and fold them into cigar shapes.
- Place the pancakes in a baking dish and bake them in an oven at 390°F for 35 minutes.
- Serve while hot.

Nutrition-Per Serving: Calories: 542Kcal, Total Fat: 35g, Total Carbs: 42g, Protein: 15g

MINI FRITTATA WITH QUINOA

There is nothing better than taking a mini frittata filled with zucchini and quinoa on a ravenous morning. Enjoy these frittatas with a cup of hot chocolate.

| Prep time: 30 min | Cook time: 30 min | Servings: 10 |

Ingredients

- ¾ cup yellow cooked quinoa
- 1 egg
- 1 egg white
- ⅓ cup shredded zucchini
- ⅓ cup Swiss cheese
- 3 tbsp diced ham
- 1 tbsp chopped parsley
- 2 ½ tbsp grated parmesan
- ⅛ tbsp white ground pepper

- *Cooking spray*

Instructions

- Mix quinoa, eggs, egg white, zucchini, Swiss cheese, ham, parsley, cheese, and pepper in a bowl until well combined.
- Preheat the oven to 390°F and grease 10 muffin tins with cooking spray.
- Spoon the muffin tins with the quinoa mixture and bake for 30 minutes.
- Allow mini frittatas to cool for 5 minutes.
- Serve while hot or cold.

Nutrition-Per Serving: Calories: 88Kcal, Total Fat: 3g, Total Carbs: 17g, Protein: 7g

HAM AND CHEESE BREAD (PRISNATS)

Have you ever prepared Prisnats before? To prepare these healthy morning delights for your family, you just need a few goods you surely have in your pantry!

| Prep time: 45 min | Cook time: 1h 5 min | Servings: 12 |

Ingredients

- 1 lb. bacon
- 1 onion, finely chopped
- 1 bunch green onions, finely chopped
- 2 tbsp yeast
- 1 cup warm water

- *12 eggs, beaten*
- *1 tbsp salt*
- *16 oz cottage cheese*
- *3 cups all-purpose flour*
- *2 tbsp cooking oil*

Instructions

- Place the bacon and the onions in a skillet and cook for 5 minutes. Drain any liquid and set it aside.
- In a bowl dissolve the yeast in warm water.
- Stir in the eggs, salt, cheese, and bacon mixture to the yeast mixture.
- Gradually stir the flour into the egg mixture until a thick batter is formed.
- Transfer the batter to a baking pan that has been greased with cooking oil.
- Preheat the oven to 350°F.
- Bake the bread for 1 hour.
- Slice and serve while warm.

Nutrition-Per Serving: Calories: 413Kcal, Total Fat: 23g, Total Carbs: 32g, Protein: 21g

SCRAMBLED EGGS WITH TRUFFLES

This is a perfect breakfast for a busy morning - you just need to toss a few ingredients to a pan and get moist and fluffy eggs on the table in less than 2o minutes.

| Prep time: 10 min | Cook time: 15 min | Servings: 2 |

Ingredients

- 2 tbsp butter
- 1 truffle
- 4 eggs
- 2 tbsp milk
- Salt and pepper to taste
- Chopped chives for garnishing

Instructions

- Slice the truffle then chop the slices into small pieces.
- Add the truffle and butter to a pan and heat over low heat for 5 minutes.
- Meanwhile, in a bowl, whisk the eggs and milk.
- Pour the egg mixture over the truffle and stir continuously until the eggs thicken.
- Cook the eggs for 4 minutes.
- Season the eggs with salt and pepper.
- Serve and garnish with chives.

Nutrition-Per Serving: Calories: 411Kcal, Total Fat: 34g, Total Carbs: 8g, Protein: 19g

SOUR CHERRY STRUDEL

This is a simple and classic tasty strudel that any vegetarian will never get enough of. It has a crispy crust and is tender on the inside.

| Prep time: 20 min | Cook time: 30 min | Servings: 6 |

Ingredients

- 21 oz cherries
- 5 tbsp golden caster sugar
- 1 lemon zest
- 3 ½ tbsp ground walnuts
- 6 phyllo sheets
- 4 tbsp melted butter
- Icing sugar for dusting

Instructions

- Preheat the oven to 390°F.
- In a bowl mix the cherries, caster sugar, lemon zest, and walnuts.
- Brush 2 phyllo sheets with 1 tablespoon of butter and align them on a flat surface.
- Scoop ⅓ of the cherry mixture onto the aligned phyllo sheets and roll to seal.
- Repeat the process for the remaining phyllo sheets.
- Transfer the cherry strudel to a greased baking pan then bake for 30 minutes.
- Allow the strudel to cool for 10 minutes.
- Dust the strudel with icing sugar and serve.

Nutrition-Per Serving: Calories: 216Kcal, Total Fat: 12g, Total Carbs: 27g, Protein: 3g

EGGPLANT WITH MARINATED FETA CHEESE

Are you looking for a crowd-pleasing dessert? This easy eggplant and cheese recipe is ideal for you. It's delicious and ideal for a Sunday barbecue.

| Prep time: 15 min | Cook time: 20 min | Servings: 6 |

Ingredients

- 1 lb. feta cheese
- 1 cup olive oil
- 2 garlic cloves
- 2 eggplants, sliced into discs
- 1 cup garlic salt
- 1 tbsp paprika

- *1 cup olive oil*

Instructions

- Crumble cheese in a mixing bowl and add oil and garlic cloves. Cover the bowl and refrigerate overnight.
- Sprinkle the eggplant discs with garlic salt.
- Mix paprika with oil and brush the mixture over the discs.
- Preheat the grill to high heat and cook the eggplant discs while brushing occasionally with the paprika mixture until golden brown on both sides.
- Top the eggplants with the cheese mix and serve.

Nutrition-Per Serving: Calories: 900Kcal, Total Fat: 84g, Total Carbs: 31g, Protein: 17g

STUFFED ARTICHOKES (PUNJENI ARTICHOKE)

These stuffed artichokes are the perfect snack to present to family or guests. It's also a terrific way to include more vegetables into your diet.

| Prep time: 30 min | Cook time: 1 h | Servings: 5 |

Ingredients

- 5 artichokes
- 1 cup breadcrumbs
- 3 garlic cloves
- ½ tbsp flat-leaf parsley
- ½ lb. baby new potatoes
- ¾ cup shelled peas

- *Salt and pepper to taste*
- *A few tbsp olive oil*

Instructions

- Remove the leaves and the stalk from the artichokes, reserving the stalks.
- Slice about 2 cm of the artichoke top and scoop the choke out with a spoon.
- In a mixing bowl, mix breadcrumbs, garlic, parsley, and pepper until well mixed.
- Open the leaves of the artichoke and stuff them with the mixture.
- Arrange the artichokes in a saucepan and add the potatoes around them.
- Scatter shelled peas and artichoke stalks on top with any remaining stuffing.
- Season well with salt and pepper. Drizzle with oil then add water until the artichokes are submerged.
- Bring to a boil, reduce heat and cook while covered for 1 hour.
- Serve and enjoy!

Nutrition-Per Serving: Calories: 530Kcal, Total Fat: 42g, Total Carbs: 37g, Protein: 9g

PUMPKIN STRUDEL (BUČNICA)

This is a popular Croatian appetizer that you should try. It's so delicious that just one piece is never enough.

| Prep time: 5 min | Cook time: 15 min | Servings: 4 |

Ingredients

- 2 lb. pumpkin, peeled and grated
- 2 tbsp salt
- ½ lb. ricotta cheese
- ½ cup sour cream
- 3 eggs
- ½ lb. phyllo dough
- Oil

Instructions

- Preheat your oven to 350F.
- Season the pumpkin with salt and let rest for 30 minutes. Squeeze with your hands to get rid of all the water.
- Mix the pumpkin with cheese, sour cream, eggs, and 1 tbsp salt.
- Place one sheet of phyllo dough on a working area and brush it with oil. Place a second sheet on the first sheet and brush it with oil.
- Add the filling on approx. ⅓ of the greased phyllo sheet and roll it into a strudel.
- Repeat the process with all phyllo sheets to make 6 rolls.
- Brush the rolls with more oil and bake in the oven for 30 minutes.
- Serve when hot.

Nutrition-Per Serving: Calories: 253Kcal, Total Fat: 11g, Total Carbs: 28g, Protein: 11g

CROATIAN PRŠUT AND ŠKRIPAVAC

This is the simplest and most ideal approach to start your meals. Pršut (dry-cured ham) and Škripavac (aged farmers' goat cheese) are locally made and can also be served as a side to other dishes.

| Prep time: 10 min | Cook time: 10 min | Servings: 4 |

Ingredients

- ½ lb. prosciutto
- ½ lb. salami, dried and cured
- ½ lb. cheese Škripavac
- ½ cup olives, green or black

Instructions

- Arrange all the ingredients neatly on a platter.
- Serve with crusty bread and some red wine.
- To spice up the plate, you can add additional types of cheese or some capers and anchovies.

Nutrition-Per Serving: Calories: 478Kcal, Total Fat: 36g, Total Carbs: 4g, Protein: 33g

LEMON OREGANO BRUSCHETTA

This is a tasty appetizer that may also double as a snack. It's really simple to make and uses ingredients you probably already have in your pantry.

Prep time: 10 min	Cook time: 0 min	Servings: 4

Ingredients

- 1 pack cream cheese
- 2 tbsp freshly chopped oregano

- *¼ tbsp salt and pepper*
- *2 tbsp lemon juice*
- *1 pack naan minis*
- *1 yellow tomato, thinly sliced*
- *1 red tomato, thinly sliced*
- *4 fresh basil leaves*
- *Olive oil (optional)*

Instructions

- In a mixing bowl, mix cream cheese, 1 tbsp oregano, salt, and pepper.
- Mix with a hand mixer for 3 minutes or until fluffy.
- Add lemon juice and mix again until well mixed. Spread the mixture over the naan minis then top with tomatoes.
- Top the tomatoes with the remaining oregano and more salt and pepper.
- Garnish with a basil leaf tared with your hands to a smaller size. If desired, drizzle with a sprinkle of olive oil.
- Serve immediately.

Nutrition-Per Serving: Calories: 246Kcal, Total Fat: 13g, Total Carbs: 28g, Protein: 6g

SOUPS AND STEWS

BROWN ROUX (PREŽGANA) SOUP

This delectable Croatian soup is eaten as a snack or for breakfast. It's simple to make, and the roux gives it a silky-smooth texture you'll enjoy.

| Prep time: 5 min | Cook time: 15 min | Servings: 4 |

Ingredients

- 1 tbsp sunflower oil
- 2 tbsp wheat flour
- 1 liter of water
- 1 egg
- Salt and pepper to taste
- 3 sprigs parsley, fresh
- White vinegar to taste
- Toasted bread pieces

Instructions

- Place oil in a saucepan and add a pinch of flour once warm.
- Whisk the remaining flour once it starts to bubble. Cook as you whisk until the roux gets smooth and thin.
- Add water and let boil for 5 minutes. Whisk in the egg and cook for a few minutes.
- Season with salt and pepper then sprinkle with parsley and toasted bread. Add 3 drops of vinegar then serve and enjoy.

Nutrition-Per Serving: Calories: 61Kcal, Total Fat: 5g, Total Carbs: 3g, Protein: 2g

CROATIAN ZAGORJE POTATO SOUP

In the northern part of Croatia, this potato soup was originally a peasant soup. It has, nonetheless, become one of Croatia's most popular soups. The soup tastes exquisite and is really addictive.

| Prep time: 5 min | Cook time: 2 h | Servings: 4 |

Ingredients

- ¾ tbsp lard
- ¾ tbsp flour
- 1 tbsp red paprika, dried
- 2 liters of water
- 0.8 lb. potatoes, cut into cubes
- ½ cup wild mushrooms, chopped
- ⅓ lb. pork ribs, dried, smoked, and sliced
- 1 bay leaf

- *6 tbsp sour cream*
- *2 tbsp dill, freshly minced*

Instructions

- Add lard in a pot and heat until it has melted. Add flour and cook until it's brownish.
- Add paprika then pour water. Stir as you remove the small flour clods.
- Add potatoes and mushrooms to the soup. Add pork and bay leaf then season with salt and pepper.
- Cook the soup for 2 hours then add sour cream and dill before serving.

Nutrition-Per Serving: Calories: 288Kcal, Total Fat: 17g, Total Carbs: 21g, Protein: 12g

MUSHROOM SOUP WITH BUCKWHEAT

The combination of mushrooms and buckwheat creates a substantial soup that will keep you warm and full throughout winter.

| Prep time: 5 min | Cook time: 35 min | Servings: 6 |

Ingredients

- *4 tbsp oil*
- *1 ½ oz onions, chopped*
- *5 oz mushrooms, fresh sliced*
- *2 garlic cloves, chopped*
- *½ cup white wine (dry)*
- *Salt and pepper to taste*
- *1 tbsp vegetable seasoning*
- *2 oz buckwheat, washed*

- *1 bay leaf*
- *2 oz sour cream*
- *Vinegar to taste*
- *Handful of parsley, chopped*

Instructions

- Heat oil on a saucepan and sauté the onions for 5 minutes, until golden.
- Add mushrooms and garlic cloves then continue to sauté for additional 2 minutes, until well coated. Pour in the wine and cook for 1-2 minutes, until the liquid has slightly evaporated.
- Season with salt, pepper, vegetable seasoning, buckwheat, and bay leaves.
- Add some water until all the ingredients are covered.
- Simmer gently for 25 minutes until the buckwheat is tender.
- Taste for seasoning and add salt and pepper, if necessary.
- Stir in sour cream, a sprinkle of vinegar, and garnish with freshly chopped parsley.

Nutrition-Per Serving: Calories: 115Kcal, Total Fat: 11g, Total Carbs: 3g, Protein: 2g

LEEK SOUP

Do you love French onion soup? This leek soup resembles it, but you don't have to cook it in the oven for finishing.

| Prep time: 25 min | Cook time: 2 h | Servings: 5 |

Ingredients

- ¾ lb. leeks
- 1 ¼ tbsp olive oil
- 1 tbsp flour
- 1 garlic clove
- 6 ⅓ cup water
- 1 ¼ tbsp salt

- *1 ¼ tbsp pepper*
- *½ lb. bread, cut into small cubes*
- *2 tbsp butter*
- *1.7 oz Swiss cheese, sliced thinly*
- *2.7 oz parmesan cheese*

Instructions

- Wash and cut leeks into rounds. Sauté them in olive oil until very tender, approx. 5-7 minutes.
- Add flour and sauté for an additional 2 minutes. Add a little water to make a sauce, stir until well combined.
- Add water and cook for 1h on medium heat.
- Add minced garlic and season the soup with salt and pepper.
- Reduce the heat to a minimum and cook for 1½ hours.
- In the meantime, cook the bread in a pan with butter until crispy, about 5 minutes.
- Add the bread to a soup bowl, cover with Swiss cheese then add the soup.
- Garnish with additional parmesan or fresh herbs, such as parsley or thyme.

Nutrition-Per Serving: Calories: 448Kcal, Total Fat: 17g, Total Carbs: 40g, Protein: 14g

PASTA AND BEAN STEW (PASTA FAZOL)

The combination of pasta and beans in a stew is ideal for a chilly day's lunch or dinner. With crusty bread and a glass of red wine, serve the entrée.

Prep time: 20 min   Cook time: 1h 45 min   Servings: 8

Ingredients

- *1 lb. white beans, soaked overnight*
- *4 bay leaves*
- *7 oz smoked pork ribs*
- *8 cups of water*
- *7 oz brown onion, chopped*
- *2 carrots, chopped*
- *4 celery stalks, chopped*
- *2 tbsp tomato paste*

- *51/2 oz smoked pancetta, chopped*
- *8 garlic cloves, finely diced*
- *3 ½ oz pasta*
- *Salt and black pepper to taste*
- *2 tbsp chopped parsley*

Instructions

- Drain the soaked beans and place them in a saucepan and add bay leaf.
- Cover the beans with water and bring them to a boil.
- In another saucepan add pork ribs, water, onions, carrot, celery, tomato paste, and pancetta then bring the mixture to a boil.
- Season the pork ribs mixture with salt and pepper and reduce the heat to low. Simmer for 1 hour.
- Remove the pancetta meat and pork ribs from the soup. Set aside.
- Add beans and garlic to the soup and cook for 30 minutes.
- Stir pasta, pancetta, pork ribs, and parsley into the beans then cook for another 5 minutes.
- Serve and enjoy.

Nutrition-Per Serving: Calories: 394Kcal, Total Fat: 30g, Total Carbs: 13g, Protein: 20g

BARLEY AND BEAN STEW

This barley and bean stew is high in fiber and so beneficial to your digestive system. It's also highly flavorful and a fantastic dinner for any ravenous day.

| Prep time: 20 min | Cook time: 1h 45 min | Servings: 6 |

Ingredients

- 4 tbsp olive oil
- 2 onions, chopped
- 2 carrots, diced
- 1 ½ cup barley porridge
- 8 ½ cups water
- Salt and black pepper to taste
- 1 bay leaf
- 2 sausages
- 1 cup of canned white beans

- *1 cup of canned red beans*

Instructions

- Heat oil in a skillet over medium heat and sauté the onions for 1 minute.
- Stir the carrots into the skillet and cook for 5 minutes.
- Stir the barley porridge to the carrot then add water until all barley is covered.
- Reduce the heat to low and simmer the barley for 1 hour.
- Season the barley with salt and pepper.
- Add the bay leaf to the stew and cook for 15 minutes.
- Stir in the beans and sausage to the barley stew and cook for 20 minutes.
- If desired, serve with a slice of fresh bread.

Nutrition-Per Serving: Calories: 497Kcal, Total Fat: 10g, Total Carbs: 84g, Protein: 20g

BEAN AND SAUSAGE STEW

Are you planning a trip to Croatia and seeking delicious cuisine to try? This hearty Smokey sausage and bean soup is exactly what you're looking for. It's full of flavor and fills you up while keeping you warm in the winter.

| Prep time: 5 min | Cook time: 45 min | Servings: 8 |

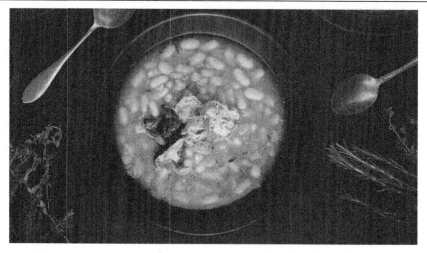

Ingredients

- 2 smoked sausages
- 3 ½ oz pancetta, diced
- 1 onion, diced
- 2 carrots, diced
- 4 garlic cloves, minced
- 15 oz cannelloni beans
- 15 oz pinto beans
- 4 tbsp tomato paste

- *1 tbsp sweet paprika*
- *1 tbsp hot paprika*
- *1 tbsp Vegeta*
- *2 cups salt stock*
- *Parsley for garnish*

Instructions

- Slice the sausages into rounds and cook them in a pan for 5 minutes.
- Add pancetta and cook until browned. Set aside and drain oil from the pan.
- Return the pan to heat and cook onions and carrots for 3 minutes then add the garlic clove. Cook until the onions are translucent.
- Add all the remaining ingredients and ensure the beans are fully covered with water. Bring to a boil.
- Reduce heat and simmer for 20 minutes. Adjust seasoning and garnish with parsley.
- Serve with hot sauce.

Nutrition-Per Serving: Calories: 331Kcal, Total Fat: 10g, Total Carbs: 40g, Protein: 22g

RABBIT STEW

Doesn't rabbit stew sound delicious? The stew contains a slew of health advantages that you won't find in fowl or meat.

| Prep time: 25 min | Cook time: 1h 40 min | Servings: 4 |

Ingredients

- ¾ cup white vinegar
- 2 cups of water
- 2 lb. rabbit, cut into 4 pieces
- 5 garlic cloves, sliced
- 8 pancetta slices
- 4 tbsp extra virgin oil
- ½ cup white wine
- 1 carrot, chopped

- *1 onion, chopped*
- *3 bay leaves*
- *1 sage sprig*
- *1 rosemary sprig*
- *1 cup chopped parsley*
- *1 lemon juice*
- *1 cups chicken stock*
- *2 tbsp caster sugar*

Instructions

- Whisk white vinegar and water in a bowl.
- Add the rabbit to the vinegar mixture and marinate it for at least 4 hours. Drain the marinade and rinse the rabbit. Dry the rabbit with a paper towel.
- Preheat the oven to 390°F.
- Make several cuts on the rabbit pieces and insert a slice of garlic into each cut.
- Wrap each rabbit piece with a pancetta slice.
- Place the rabbit on a roasting pan and pour over 3 tbsp of oil and white wine. Roast the rabbit for 30 minutes
- Meanwhile, heat the remaining oil in a pan over medium heat.
- Sauté the carrots and onions for 8 minutes.
- Stir bay leaf, sage, rosemary, rosemary, lemon juice, chicken stock, and sugar to the carrot and bring the mixture to a boil.
- Pour the seasoned mixture over the rabbit and roast at 350°F for 1 hour. Serve and enjoy!

Nutrition-Per Serving: Calories: 638Kcal, Total Fat: 27g, Total Carbs: 23g, Protein: 71g

BEEF AND HORSE STEW (COBANAC)

On a cold day, Cobanac stew is the perfect comfort food. The beef is nicely encased in a delicious wine sauce. This is a dish that will keep your visitors coming back for more.

| Prep time: 30 min | Cook time: 2 h 40 min | Servings: 6 |

Ingredients

- ½ oz dried mushroom
- 1 tbsp lard
- 21 oz onions, finely chopped
- 10 ½ oz beef, cut into small pieces
- 10 ½ oz horse meat, cut into small pieces
- 1 tbsp sweet paprika

- *1 tbsp hot paprika*
- *Salt and black pepper to taste*
- *1 bay leaf*
- *5 oz smoked pancetta, cut into small pieces*
- *½ tbsp dried thyme*
- *1 cup white wine*
- *17 ½ oz potatoes, diced*
- *3 cups of water*

Instructions

- Soak the mushrooms in cold water for 15 minutes then cut them into small pieces.
- Heat the lard in a skillet over medium heat and sauté the onions for 3 minutes.
- Stir in beef and horse meat to the skillet and cook them for 20 minutes.
- Stir in paprika, salt, pepper, bay leaf, pancetta, and thyme to the meat then cook for about 5 minutes.
- Stir in white wine to the meat and cook for 10 minutes until almost all the liquid has evaporated.
- Stir in the potatoes and water to the meat and cook on low heat for 2 hours.
- If desired, serve with some freshly chopped parsley.

Nutrition-Per Serving: Calories: 347Kcal, Total Fat: 14g, Total Carbs: 28g, Protein: 27g

LAMB STEW WITH GREEN PEAS

If you're seeking for a delicious lamb dinner, this is the recipe for you. This lamb stew will not only fill you up, but it will also nourish you.

| Prep time: 30 min | Cook time: 1h 30 min | Servings: 4 |

Ingredients

- *2 tbsp olive oil*
- *9 oz chopped onions, finely chopped*
- *1 ½ lb. lamb, cut into smaller pieces*
- *2 tbsp paprika*
- *½ tbsp thyme*
- *Salt and black pepper to taste*
- *1 cup white wine*
- *3 cups of water*

- *14 oz green peas*
- *7 oz potato, peeled and diced*
- *1 carrot, chopped*
- *Roughly chopped parsley for topping*

Instructions

- Heat oil in a skillet over medium heat and sauté the onions for 3 minutes.
- Stir in the lamb and cook it for 20 minutes.
- Stir paprika, thyme, salt, pepper, and white wine to the lamb.
- Cook the lamb for 10 minutes until almost all the liquid has evaporated.
- Add water to the lamb and cook for 30 minutes.
- Stir in the peas, potatoes, and carrots to the stew and cook for 20 minutes.
- Serve the lamb stew topped with some freshly chopped parsley.

Nutrition-Per Serving: Calories: 613Kcal, Total Fat: 36g, Total Carbs: 25g, Protein: 47g

BUTTERNUT SQUASH STEW

Cold weather necessitates a hearty stew. This butternut squash recipe offers a flavorful lunch that will keep you full all day.

| Prep time: 1h 20 min | Cook time: 25 min | Servings: 4 |

Ingredients

- 2 lb. butternut squash, diced
- 3 ½ oz onions, chopped
- 2 tbsp vinegar
- 1 ½ tbsp lard
- 1 tbsp flour
- 1 tbsp paprika

- *8 tbsp of water*
- *1 cup sour cream*
- *Cooked pasta*

Instructions

- Add butternut, salt, and vinegar to a bowl and marinate for 1 hour.
- Heat the lard in a skillet over medium heat and sauté the onions for 3 minutes.
- Stir in the flour and cook for 1 minute.
- Stir in paprika and water to the skillet and cook for 2 minutes.
- Drain excess liquid from the butternut pieces and add them to the skillet.
- Cook the butternut for 15 minutes.
- Stir sour cream into the butternut stew and remove them from heat.
- Serve the butternut stew with pasta.

Nutrition-Per Serving: Calories: 200Kcal, Total Fat: 7g, Total Carbs: 35g, Protein: 4g

MAIN DISHES RECIPES

BLACK RISOTTO

Food that is black in color is quite rare. The cuttlefish ink gives the risotto the black color without changing the taste of this delicacy.

| Prep time: 30 min | Cook time: 1h | Servings: 4 |

Ingredients

- *7 tbsp extra virgin olive oil*
- *2 tbsp chopped garlic*
- *7 oz brown onions, chopped*
- *2 lb. cuttlefish, cleaned and cut into smaller pieces*
- *Salt and black pepper to taste*

- *1 tbsp tomato paste*
- *3 ½ oz white wine*
- *2 ½ cup fish stock*
- *½ tbsp cuttlefish ink*
- *10 ½ oz risotto rice*

Instructions

- Heat oil in a pan over medium heat and sauté garlic for 1 minute. Stir onions into the garlic and sauté for about 4 minutes.
- Stir in the cuttlefish, salt, and pepper to the garlic and sauté it for about 10 minutes until all the liquid evaporates.
- Stir the tomato sauce to the cuttlefish and cook for 2 minutes.
- Pour white wine over the cuttlefish and cook for about 5 minutes until most of the liquid evaporates.
- Stir in the fish stock and cuttlefish ink then simmer for 10 minutes.
- Stir the rice into the cuttlefish and cook for 16 minutes, stirring constantly.
- Serve while hot. If desired, sprinkle some parmesan cheese over the dish.

Nutrition-Per Serving: Calories: 358Kcal, Total Fat: 14g, Total Carbs: 16g, Protein: 42g

BAKED STRUKLI

Begin your day with these Strukli. A mouthwatering filling is surrounded by soft-baked dough. It is very likely that it will become a favorite of your children.

| Prep time: 30 min | Cook time: 45 min | Servings: 4 |

Ingredients

For the Dough

- 4 cups all-purpose flour
- 1 tbsp salt
- 1 egg
- 2 tbsp sunflower oil
- 1 tbsp vinegar
- ½ cup lukewarm water
- Butter

For the filling

- 20 oz cottage cheese
- 3 ½ oz softened butter

- *4 eggs*
- *½ cup sour cream*
- *Salt and black pepper to taste*

For the topping

- *Sour cream*
- *Cheddar cheese, grated*

Instructions

- In a bowl, add flour and salt and stir. Once combined, add the egg and oil to the flour mixture and stir until well combined.
- Add water and vinegar and knead until the dough is smooth.
- Divide the dough into 3 parts and leave it covered for 30 minutes to rest.
- Meanwhile, prepare the filling by mixing all the filling ingredients in a bowl.
- Roll out the dough on a flat surface until thin. Stretch out the dough using your hand. Try not to break it.
- Brush the dough with butter then scoops ⅓ of the filling onto each part of the dough – spread evenly. Roll the dough over the filling and tuck the end to seal. Repeat the process for the remaining dough. Cut the dough into 4-inch pieces.
- Preheat the oven to 395°F and coat the baking pan with butter.
- Mix the filling ingredients in a bowl and place the Strukli on the pan. Pour the filling over the Strukli and bake for 45 minutes.
- Serve and enjoy.

Nutrition-Per Serving: Calories: 485Kcal, Total Fat: 46g, Total Carbs: 17g, Protein: 7g

FRIED SQUID RINGS (PRŽENI LIGNJI)

Squid rings make a delicious Serbian main course. They are very easy to put together yet very delicious.

| Prep time: 15 min | Cook time: 30 min | Servings: 2 |

Ingredients

- 34 oz cooking oil
- 1 cup flour
- 1 spoon red pepper powder
- 2 lb. squid, fresh and cut into the ring pieces
- 1 lemon wedges
- Salt to taste

Directions

- Pour oil into a saucepan and heat it at medium heat.

- In a mixing bowl, mix flour and pepper powder.
- Roll the squids in the flour mixture and lower the heat to low and cook the squids in oil for 10 minutes.
- Remove squids from oil and place them on paper towels to absorb excess oil.
- Serve and enjoy.

Nutrition- Per Serving: Calories: 646kcal, Total Fat: 7g, Carbs: 62g, Protein: 77g

FUZI

This spaghetti meal can be made as a comfortable dinner any day of the week. It will leave you with a delectable taste that you will not be able to forget.

| Prep time: 30 min | Cook time: 35 min | Servings: 4 |

Ingredients

- *2 cups bread flour*
- *Salt to taste*
- *2 eggs*
- *1 tbsp oil*
- *2 tbsp white wine*
- *¾ cup water*

For the Beef Sauces

- 1 tbsp olive oil
- 2 garlic cloves
- 1 tbsp red pepper
- 2 cups tomato sauce
- ½ tbsp rosemary
- 3 ½ oz beef, cut into small pieces
- Black pepper to taste

Instructions

- Sift flour and salt in a bowl. Stir in eggs, oil, and wine to the flour mixture.
- Gradually add water to the flour and knead to a smooth dough.
- Roll out the dough into a ¼ -inch thickness then cut it into 1 ½ inch square.
- Place a wooden spoon handle over the dough and fold opposite ends over each other (or just fold with your hands).
- Press the dough with a finger to stick the edges together.
- Repeat the folding process with all the dough.
- Cook the dough in boiling and salted water for 2-3 minutes.
- Meanwhile, pour oil into a saucepan and sauté garlic and red pepper for 2 minutes. Stir in the tomato sauce, rosemary, beef, salt, and pepper then cook for 30 minutes.
- Serve the Fuzi and the sauce while hot.

Nutrition-Per Serving: Calories: 399Kcal, Total Fat: 19g, Total Carbs: 38g, Protein: 14g

GRILLED OCTOPUS (HOBOTNICA NA ZARU)

You might assume that prepping octopus is difficult. Believe me when I say that this is the simplest dinner you can make for your family. You'll have them licking their lips.

| Prep time: 20 min | Cook time: 3h 15 min | Servings: 6 |

Ingredients

- *1 ¾ lb. octopus*
- *1 bunch rosemary*
- *1 bunch oregano*
- *½ cup white wine*
- *3 tbsp olive oil*
- *1 tbsp chili flakes*
- *1 tbsp paprika powder*
- *2 garlic cloves, finely grated*
- *Salt and black pepper to taste*

For garnishing

- *Fresh rosemary*
- *1 lemon, thinly sliced*
- *Handful cherry tomatoes*

Instructions

- Preheat the oven to 210°F.
- Place the octopus in salty boiling water and cook for 3 minutes.
- Drain excess water from the octopus and set it aside.
- Place the rosemary and oregano on the bottom of a casserole dish then layer the octopus on top.
- Pour wine over the octopus and cook in the oven for 3 hours.
- Meanwhile mix olive oil, chili, paprika, garlic, salt, and pepper in a bowl. Set aside.
- Cut off the octopus tentacles and head. Cut the head into two.
- Add the tentacles and head in the oil mix and toss to coat.
- Heat the chargrill over high heat.
- Shake excess oil from the octopus and grill it for 5 minutes on each side.
- Toss the octopus in the oil mixture and serve with rosemary and lemon slices and a few cherry tomatoes.
- Serve with some fresh summer salad.

Nutrition-Per Serving: Calories: 185Kcal, Total Fat: 9g, Total Carbs: 6g, Protein: 21g

GRILLED SARDINES WITH SWISS CHARD AND POTATOES

Sardines, despite their small size, are high in omega-3 fatty acids, making them a nutritious seafood option for you and your children. They are inexpensive and have a delicious flavor, especially when grilled.

| Prep time: 1h 10 min | Cook time: 40 min | Servings: 4 |

Ingredients

- 8 sardines, descaled and gutted
- 6 tbsp olive oil
- 3 minced garlic cloves
- 3 tbsp chopped parsley
- 3 cups chopped, cooked potatoes
- Salt to taste
- 1 tbsp roughly chopped dill
- 1 bunch Swiss chard

- *3 tbsp yellow onions*
- *1 lemon juice*
- *Freshly ground black pepper to taste*
- *1 tomato, cut into wedges*
- *Chopped fresh rosemary for garnishing*

Instructions

- In a bowl, toss sardines, 2 tbsp of olive oil, half of the garlic, and 1 tbsp of parsley. Marinate for 1 hour in a refrigerator.
- Cook and cut the potatoes into small chunks. In a bowl, toss the potatoes, salt, 2 tbsp of olive oil, remaining parsley, and dill. Set aside.
- Boil Swiss chard in salty water for 2 minutes. Transfer to cold water and let stand for 1 min. Remove the chard from the water.
- Heat the remaining oil in a skillet over medium heat and sauté onion, remaining garlic, and Swiss chard for 3 minutes.
- Stir in the lemon juice, salt, and pepper to the chard then remove the skillet from heat. Set aside.
- Place the sardines on a preheated griddle pan and grill for 3 minutes per side. Season the sardine with salt and pepper.
- Serve the sardines with Swiss chard, potatoes, tomato wedges and garnished with fresh rosemary.

Nutrition-Per Serving: Calories: 337Kcal, Total Fat: 23g, Total Carbs: 24g, Protein: 9g

OCTOPUS PEKA

To replace the traditional method of roasting meat under a metal dome surrounded by coal, a heavy casserole dish is employed. The end product is a mouthwatering feast that will leave you wanting more.

| Prep time: 45 min | Cook time: 2h 30 min | Servings: 8 |

Ingredients

- *4 lb. octopus, cleaned*
- *1 cup extra virgin olive oil*
- *4 minced garlic cloves*
- *3 lb. peeled potatoes, cut into quarters*
- *10 shallots*

- *4 carrots cut lengthwise*
- *Salt and black pepper to taste*
- *1 lemon juice*
- *6 rosemary sprigs*
- *1 cup dry white wine*

Instructions

- Cook the octopus in boiling water for 1 hour.
- Drain excess water from the octopus and cut it into smaller pieces.
- Preheat the oven to 425°F.
- In a bowl mix ¼ of the oil with garlic. Set aside.
- Lay the potatoes in the bottom of a casserole dish and pour the remaining oil over the potatoes.
- Add the roughly cut shallot, carrots, and octopus to the casserole then season with salt and pepper.
- Pour the garlic oil and lemon juice over the octopus and lay the rosemary on top. Cover the dish and put it in the oven.
- Bake the octopus for 45 minutes.
- Lift the lid and stir the content, and pour white wine on top.
- Cook the Peka uncovered for additional 25 minutes.
- Serve and enjoy.

Nutrition-Per Serving: Calories: 500Kcal, Total Fat: 17g, Total Carbs: 44g, Protein: 42g

HAM WITH CHESTNUTS

The ham and chestnuts are perfectly cooked to make a delectable supper. Furthermore, chestnuts are high in antioxidants, making them extremely beneficial.

| Prep time: 10 min | Cook time: 1h 30 min | Servings: 4 |

Ingredients

- *1 tbsp olive oil*
- *1 lb. smoked pork legs, cut into slices*
- *1 garlic clove, thinly sliced*
- *5 oz leek, chopped*
- *1 tbsp balsamic vinegar*
- *1 cup dry red wine vinegar*
- *1 rosemary sprig*

- *2 cups chicken stocks*
- *Salt and black pepper to taste*
- *7 oz chestnuts*
- *Steamed asparagus*

Instructions

- Heat oil in a pan over medium heat and sear the pork for 1 minute on each side.
- Remove the pork from the pan and set it aside.
- Sauté the garlic and the leek for 3 minutes.
- Add vinegar, red wine, and rosemary to the pan and ignite the wine with a flame.
- Add the pork to the pan as soon as the flame extinguishes and pour over the chicken stock.
- Season the pork with salt and pepper then simmer for 50 minutes.
- Turn the pork slices and spoon the chestnuts over them.
- Cook the pork for 20 minutes.
- Serve the ham with steamed asparagus.

Nutrition-Per Serving: Calories: 884Kcal, Total Fat: 20g, Total Carbs: 30g, Protein: 134g

CHICKEN PAPRIKA WITH SOUR CREAM

This is a fragrant, sour cream-enhanced dish unlike any other. It is soft, creamy and it melts in your mouth.

| Prep time: 10 min | Cook time: 1h 20 min | Servings: 4 |

Ingredients

- ¾ tbsp olive oil
- 2 finely chopped onion
- 2 ¼ lb. chicken breasts, with skin
- ¾ cups white wine
- 3 tbsp paprika
- ¼ tbsp chili
- ½ tbsp salt

- *1 tbsp black pepper*
- *½ tbsp caraway seeds*
- *1 tomato, sliced*
- *1 tbsp chopped parsley*
- *1 ¼ cup water*
- *3 tbsp sour cream*

Instructions

- Heat oil in a skillet over medium heat and sauté the onions for 3 minutes.
- Stir in the chicken and sauté for 5 minutes.
- Pour wine over the chicken and cook for 5 minutes.
- Stir in paprika, chili, salt, pepper, caraway seeds, tomato, parsley, and water to the chicken and simmer for 50 minutes.
- Stir in sour cream to the chicken and cook for 5 minutes.
- Serve with some mashed potatoes or rice and enjoy!

Nutrition-Per Serving: Calories: 553Kcal, Total Fat: 28g, Total Carbs: 18g, Protein: 56g

GRILLED CHICKEN

The grilled chicken is tender and juicy. Furthermore, grilling takes only a few minutes. You'll like taking it on its own or with your favorite salad.

| Prep time: 4 h 10 min | Cook time: 10 min | Servings: 4 |

Ingredients

- *1 lb. chicken breast*
- *¼ cup extra virgin olive oil*
- *¼ cup fresh lemon juice*
- *Salt and black pepper to taste*
- *1 lemon, cut into wedges*
- *Oregano for garnishing*

Instructions

- Butterfly the chicken breast and pound them into ½ -inch thickness using a meat mallet.
- Whisk olive oil and lemon juice in a bowl.
- Add the chicken breast to the bowl and marinate them for at least 4 hours.
- Heat the grill to high heat.
- Grill the chicken to high heat for 4 minutes on each side.
- Serve the chicken with lemon wedges and garnish with oregano.

Nutrition-Per Serving: Calories: 255Kcal, Total Fat: 16g, Total Carbs: 2g, Protein: 24g

STUFFED BELL PEPPERS

I'm curious how many people enjoy leftover foods. I, too, dislike them. These stuffed peppers are a great way to use up leftover rice while also providing a one-pot finger-licking supper.

| Prep time: 15 min | Cook time: 1h 15 min | Servings: 10 |

Ingredients

- 10 yellow bell peppers
- 1lb ground beef
- 1 finely chopped onion
- 2 minced garlic cloves
- 1 egg
- 2 tbsp rice
- Salt and black pepper to taste

- *2 cups tomato sauce*
- *Chopped rosemary for topping*

For the Roux

- *4 tbsp oil*
- *4 tbsp all-purpose flour*

Instructions

- Clean the peppers and cut off the tops. Discard the pepper tops.
- Remove seeds from the bell peppers.
- In a bowl mix ground beef, onion, garlic, egg, rice, salt, and pepper.
- Stuff the peppers with the ground beef mixture.
- Prepare a roux by heating oil in a skillet over medium heat.
- Gradually add flour to the oil and cook for 2 minutes while stirring constantly.
- Place the stuffed peppers in a separate skillet and pour over the tomato sauce.
- Cook the stuffed peppers for 1 hour on low heat.
- Pour the roux over the peppers and cook for 10 minutes.
- Serve the stuffed peppers and top with rosemary.

Nutrition-Per Serving: Calories: 266Kcal, Total Fat: 12g, Total Carbs: 23g, Protein: 16g

SHRIMP RISOTTO

Are you seeking a delectable seafood dish to provide to your family? This shrimp risotto is full of rich flavors and ideal for a hectic weekday.

| Prep time: 15 min | Cook time: 35 min | Servings: 4 |

Ingredients

- 2 tbsp extra virgin olive oil
- 1 onion, finely chopped
- 1 garlic clove, minced
- 14 oz shrimp tail, peeled and deveined
- ½ cup dry white wine
- 11 oz rice
- 2 ½ tbsp tomato paste
- 6 ¼ cup fish stock
- 1 tbsp chopped parsley

- *1 ¼ tbsp butter*
- *Salt and black pepper to taste*

Instructions

- Heat oil in a skillet over medium heat and sauté the onions and garlic for 3 minutes.
- Stir in the shrimps to the skillet and cook for 5 minutes, tossing them occasionally.
- Add wine to the shrimps and cook for 10 minutes until almost all the liquid has evaporated.
- Stir the rice and tomato paste into the shrimp.
- Pour the fish stock over the shrimp and cook for 15 minutes, stirring occasionally.
- Stir in parsley, butter, salt, and pepper to shrimp then serve.

Nutrition-Per Serving: Calories: 333Kcal, Total Fat: 15g, Total Carbs: 17g, Protein: 33g

CROATIAN MUSSELS (DAGNJE NA BUZARU)

This succulent and easy-to-make mussel recipe will be your new family favorite. The genius behind perfectly cooked mussels is adding a moderate amount of salt, or no salt at all, since mussels are naturally salty.

| Prep time: 20 min | Cook time: 20 min | Servings: 4 |

Ingredients

- 4 lb. mussels
- ¾ cup olive oil
- ¼ cup parsley, freshly chopped
- 8 garlic cloves, chopped
- 1 ¼ cups dry white wine
- Small pinch of sea salt
- Black pepper
- ¾ cup breadcrumbs

Directions

- Scrub and debeard mussels and add them to a skillet over medium heat. Discard all mussels which are open – they are not alive and therefore no good to cook.
- Add oil, parsley, and garlic to the skillet. Simmer until the mussels start to open. Reduce heat and add wine, salt, and pepper.
- Cook while stirring occasionally until all the shells are open. Discard any mussels that did not open during cooking – they are no good. Increase the heat to high to cook the mussels faster.
- Mix breadcrumbs into the broth, ensuring you leave some liquid present.
- Serve with some crusty bread and enjoy.

Nutrition- Per Serving: Calories: 681kcal, Total Fat: 3g, Carbs: 139g, Protein: 23g

CROATIAN BUZARA SHRIMPS

Buzara shrimp is the easiest way to prepare a light and finger-licking dinner in just 30 minutes. More so, shrimps are packed with numerous nutrients that are of great health benefits.

| Prep time: 25 min | Cook time: 30 min | Servings: 4 |

Ingredients

- 4 tbsp olive oil
- 2 minced garlic cloves
- 35 oz shrimp
- 2 cups white wine
- ½ cup tomatoes, strained
- ¼ tbsp salt
- ½ oz raisins
- Black pepper to taste

- *½ oz breadcrumbs*
- *1 cup minced parsley*

Directions

- Heat oil in a skillet and sauté garlic for 30 seconds.
- Stir in the shrimp to the skillet.
- Add wine to the shrimp and cook for 5 minutes until all the wine evaporates.
- Stir in tomato, salt, raisins, pepper, and bread crumbs to the shrimp.
- Cook the shrimp covered for 20 minutes.
- Stir in the parsley to the shrimp and serve.

Nutrition - per serving: Calories: 504kcal, Total fat: 17g, Carbs: 11g, Protein: 54g

SWISS CHARD AND POTATOES

This delectable dish will wow your vegan friends. It's filling while only requiring 5 cupboard ingredients.

| Prep time: 10 min | Cook time: 20 min | Servings: 2 |

Ingredients

- *3 potatoes, peeled and cut into small pieces*
- *5 tbsp olive oil*
- *5 garlic cloves, thinly sliced*
- *1 bunch Swiss chard, stalks removed and cut into strips*
- *Salt and pepper to taste*

Instructions

- Boil the potatoes in salty water for 6 minutes.

- Drain excess water from the potatoes and set aside.
- Heat oil in a skillet and sauté the garlic for 2 minutes.
- Stir the potatoes into the skillet and cook for 7 minutes.
- Add chard, salt, and pepper to the potatoes then toss to mix.
- Cook the chard for 4 minutes.
- Serve the chard and potatoes while hot.

Nutrition-Per Serving: Calories: 379Kcal, Total Fat: 17g, Total Carbs: 52g, Protein: 7g

SALAD RECIPES

TOMATO AND ONION VINEGAR SALAD

This salad is ideal during the summer or when tomatoes are in season. It's a simple but tasty side dish to offer with grilled fish.

| Prep time: 10 min | Cook time: 0 min | Servings: 4 |

Ingredients

- 5 tomatoes, thinly sliced
- 1 onion, thinly sliced
- 3 tbsp red wine vinegar
- 3 tbsp extra virgin olive oil
- Salt and pepper to taste

Instructions

- Add the sliced tomatoes to a flat bowl then add the onions on the tomatoes.
- Add the red wine vinegar and oil.
- Season with salt and pepper to taste then toss until well combined.
- Serve and enjoy.

Nutrition-Per Serving: Calories: 131Kcal, Total Fat: 11g, Total Carbs: 8g, Protein: 2g

MIXED SALAD

This is a popular salad in Croatia, and you can find it in virtually every family, especially during the summer. The secret component is vinegar, usually homemade, which keeps you hydrated on hot days.

| Prep time: 10 min | Cook time: 0 min | Servings: 3 |

Ingredients

- ½ lb. tomatoes
- 2 medium green bell peppers
- 2 medium cucumbers
- 2 onions
- 2 tbsp vinegar
- 1 tbsp olive oil

- *Salt and pepper to taste*
- *1 tbsp chopped Feta cheese*
- *Fresh herbs for garnish*

Instructions

- Slice the tomatoes into 8 pieces.
- Slice the green peppers into thin slices.
- Peel the cucumber and slice it into thin pieces.
- Cut the onions into thin slices.
- Add all the ingredients to a mixing bowl, add the vinegar, oil, salt, and pepper then toss until combined.
- Let cool in the fridge for 30 minutes. Serve garnished with feta cheese and fresh herbs, such as basil, thyme or parsley.

Nutrition-Per Serving: Calories: 320Kcal, Total Fat: 20g, Total Carbs: 26g, Protein: 7g

CABBAGE WITH YOGHURT DRESSING

If you're looking for a salad recipe that will please everyone, this cabbage with yogurt dressing is a terrific option. It turns out brightly colored and flavorful. Just before serving, toss the salad with the dressing.

| Prep time: 5 min | Cook time: 0 min | Servings: 2 |

Ingredients

- *¼ cabbage*
- *2 carrots*
- *1 onion*
- *2 tbsp olive oil*
- *1 Greek yogurt*
- *Salt to taste*
- *1 tbsp lemon juice*

- *Balsamic vinegar*

Instructions

- Slice the cabbage thinly, grate the carrots and slice the onions thinly.
- Add the ingredients to a mixing bowl and drizzle olive oil
- Prepare the dressing by mixing yogurt, lemon juice, vinegar, and salt to taste.
- Toss the salad with the dressing and serve immediately. Enjoy.

Nutrition-Per Serving: Calories: 320Kcal, Total Fat: 20g, Total Carbs: 26g, Protein: 7g

FRENCH BEANS SALAD

Croatian French bean salad is so tasty that it leaves your taste buds tantalized. Even better, you may use flat, round, green, or yellow French beans which are all easy to make.

| Prep time: 15 min | Cook time: 30 min | Servings: 3 |

Ingredients

- ⅕ French beans
- 1 garlic clove
- 1 tbsp oil
- 1 tbsp vinegar
- ½ tbsp salt
- ⅛ tbsp pepper
- 2 tbsp water

Directions

- Clean the French beans and cut them into large pieces.
- Cook the beans in hot water for 10 minutes. Change the water and cook until soft.
- Drain the beans and transfer them to a salad bowl.
- Add garlic, oil, and vinegar. Season everything with salt and pepper.
- Let cool and serve when cold.

Nutrition- Per Serving: Calories: 386kcal, Total Fat: 7g, Carbs: 65g, Protein: 19g

OCTOPUS SALAD (SALATA OD HOBOTNICE)

There is nothing amazing like this octopus salad. Its satisfying and packed with both flavors and nutrients. Always use frozen octopus as freezing it relaxes its mussels. Fresh octopus is a little chewy once cooked and not pleasant to eat.

| Prep time: 25 min | Cook time: 35 min | Servings: 4 |

Ingredients

- 2lb octopus, frozen for 2 days
- 7 oz Nicola potatoes, skin in
- 2 bay leaves
- 10 peppercorns
- ⅓ cup extra virgin olive oil
- 1 ¼ oz red wine vinegar
- ½ finely chopped red onion
- 7 oz cherry tomatoes, halved

- *2 sliced cucumbers*
- *2 chopped garlic cloves*
- *2 tbsp chopped parsley*
- *Salt and black pepper to taste*

Directions

- Tenderize the octopus by defrosting it, then beat it with a mallet.
- Add the potatoes to a skillet of boiling salted water and cook them for 20 minutes.
- Drain the water and allow the potatoes to cool then cut them into ½ inch slices.
- Meanwhile, add the bay leaves, peppercorns, water to a skillet and bring to a boil.
- Add the octopus to the boiling water and cook it for 12 minutes.
- Drain the water and allow the octopus to cool for about 5 minutes.
- Skin the octopus and cut its tentacles into ¼ inch slices.
- In a dish mix the octopus, the potatoes, oil, vinegar, onion, tomatoes, cucumber, garlic, parsley, salt, and pepper until well combined.
- Serve while warm.

Nutrition - per serving: Calories: 340kcal, Total fat: 10g, Carbs: 25g, Protein: 36g

FRESH CUCUMBER SALAD

This is a delicious and refreshing salad to serve during hot weather. The salad is crunchy and is a perfect accompaniment to grilled fish or meat. If you wish to add some more flavor, add in some sliced onion.

| Prep time: 5 min | Cook time: 0 min | Servings: 6 |

Ingredients

- *7 oz cucumber*
- *1 garlic clove, minced*
- *1 tbsp vinegar*
- *1 tbsp oil*
- *½ tbsp salt*
- *¼ tbsp black pepper*
- *3 tbsp water*

Directions

- Peel the cucumber and slice them into rings.
- In a bowl, toss the cucumber, garlic, vinegar, oil, salt, pepper, and water.
- Cool in a refrigerator before serving.

Nutrition - per serving: Calories: 158kcal, Total fat: 14g, Carbs: 9g, Protein: 2g

SIMPLE BEAN SALAD

This is a delightful salad that can be made in large quantities and stored in the refrigerator for up to three days. The best part is that you may use any sort of beans you want, not just brown.

| Prep time: 5 min | Cook time: 0 min | Servings: 4 |

Ingredients

- ½ lb. beans (or canned beans)
- 2 onions
- ½ cup water
- 2 tbsp vinegar
- 2 tbsp oil
- 2 tbsp salt
- 2 tbsp pepper

Instructions

- Cook the beans until very soft. Drain the beans and transfer them to your salad bowl. You could skip this step if you decided to use canned beans.
- Thinly slice the onions and add to the beans.
- Season well with salt and pepper.
- In a separate mixing bowl, mix water and vinegar then pour over the salad.
- Mix well then pour oil and stir well.
- Refrigerate for at least 1 hour. Season with salt and pepper to taste then serve.

Nutrition-Per Serving: Calories: 320Kcal, Total Fat: 20g, Total Carbs: 26g, Protein: 7g

FRENCH SALAD (FRANCUSKA SALATA)

This is a tasty salad that is irresistible and perfect for Christmas and New Year celebrations. It is prepared and eaten all over Croatia (in slightly different variations) and traditionally accompanies major holiday feasts.

Prep time: 25 min   Cook time: 25 min   Servings: 6

Ingredients

- 7 oz boiled potatoes, skin removed
- 3 ½ oz gherkins
- 2 celery stalks
- 7 oz carrots
- 3 hard-boiled eggs
- 1 green apple, skin removed
- 4 cups of water
- 8 ¾ oz frozen peas

For the Dressing

- *10 ½ oz whole egg mayonnaise*
- *1 ½ tbsp lemon juice*
- *1 tbsp smooth mustard*
- *White pepper to taste*
- *Salt to taste*

Directions

- Chop the potatoes, gherkins, celery stalks, carrots, eggs, and apples into similar-sized cubes.
- Pour water into a saucepan and bring it to a boil.
- Add the peas to the saucepan and cook for 15 minutes.
- Add the carrots and celery to the peas and cook for another 10 minutes.
- Drain the excess water from the peas and allow them to cool.
- In a salad bowl mix the potatoes, gherkins, eggs, apple, and the pea mixture.
- In another bowl mix all the dressing ingredients.
- Pour the dressing over the salad and toss to mix.
- Refrigerate the salad for 2 hours before serving.

Nutrition - per serving: Calories: 505kcal, Total fat: 22g, Carbs: 47g, Protein: 31g

DESSERT RECIPES

PAPRENJACI (GINGERBREAD COOKIES)

Are you a fan of gingerbread cookies? This is a sort of Croatian gingerbread cookie that is heavily flavored with black pepper. It turns out really tasty, resulting in a great cookie.

| Prep time: 15 min | Cook time: 15 min | Servings: 20 |

Ingredients

- *2 sticks butter*
- *1 tbsp pork fat*
- *2 eggs*
- *1 ¼ cups sugar*
- *¾ cup honey*
- *3 ¾ cups walnuts*
- *3 tbsp cinnamon, ground*

- *1 tbsp nutmeg*
- *1 tbsp pepper, ground*
- *5 pieces cloves, ground*
- *1 pinch cardamom*
- *7 cups flour*
- *1 lemon peel*

Instructions

- In a mixing bowl, whisk together butter and pork fat until foamy.
- Add all other ingredients except the flour and mix well.
- Add the flour little by little while mixing until the mixture starts to fall off your fingers.
- Wrap the dough in cling film and let it rest in the fridge for up to 2 hours.
- Transfer the dough between 2 parchment papers and roll it out while flipping it several times.
- Use a cookie cutter to cut the cookies or a traditional wooden mold and press it on the mold then use a knife to cut the cookies.
- Place the cookies on a greased baking sheet and bake in the oven for 12 minutes at 350F.
- Serve the cookies and enjoy.

Nutrition-Per Serving: Calories: 242Kcal, Total Fat: 12g, Total Carbs: 30g, Protein: 5g

FRITULE

Fritule can be served as a dessert and as a welcoming dish. They come out delicious and moist from the inside while crunchy on the outside.

| Prep time: 20 min | Cook time: 50 min | Servings: 4 |

Ingredients

- *2 potatoes*
- *⅔ Sultanas (or other types of raisins)*
- *¼ cup dark rum*
- *1 lemon rind, grated*
- *1 orange, grated*
- *¼ tbsp nutmeg, ground*
- *1 tbsp vanilla extract*
- *1 ¼ cups caster sugar*
- *2 eggs, beaten*
- *1 ½ cups plain flour*
- *2 tbsp yeast*
- *⅓ cup water*

- *Vegetable oil for frying*

Instructions

- Add potatoes to a deep saucepan and add water. Barring to a boil then reduce heat to simmer for 40 minutes or until tender. Drain the potatoes and set them aside.
- Meanwhile, add raisins and rum in another saucepan. Bring to a boil, remove from heat and let soak for 20 minutes.
- Return the potatoes to the saucepan and mash with lemon rinds, orange, nutmeg, vanilla, and sugar until very smooth.
- Add the soaked raisins, eggs, flour, yeast, and water. Stir until a thick and smooth batter is formed.
- Cover and set aside for 1 hour.
- Fill a deep fryer with ⅓ of oil and heat over medium heat. Drop a tablespoon of the batter in the hot oil and cool while turning until golden brown.
- Remove the donuts with a slotted spoon and drain them on a paper towel.
- Roll in caster sugar and serve.

Nutrition-Per Serving: Calories: 55Kcal, Total Fat: 0.3g, Total Carbs: 12g, Protein: 1g

ŠNENOKLE

Are you looking for a crowd-pleasing dessert to present to your visitors or during family gatherings? This is the recipe you're looking for. The Šnenokle is so delicious that cooking it just once will not suffice.

| Prep time: 5 min | Cook time: 0 min | Servings: 4 |

Ingredients

- 4 *eggs*
- 100g *biscuits*
- 1 *tbsp rum*
- 2 *cups Milk*
- 5 *tbsp sugar*
- 2 *tbsp vanilla extract*
- 1 *tbsp dark chocolate (optional)*
- 1 *pinch salt*

Instructions

- Beat the egg whites in a mixing bowl with salt until stiff peaks form.
- Break up the biscuits and add them to the dessert bowl. Sprinkle them with rum.
- Add milk and vanilla sugar to a saucepan and bring the mixture to a boil.
- Place a heaped spoonful of egg whites on the milk mixture and let them cook for 30 seconds on each side.
- Arrange the egg whites on the biscuits.
- In a separate bowl, whisk the egg yolks and add the hot milk to it. Stir gently and bring the mixture to a boil until thickened.
- Pour the mixture around the egg whites and over the biscuits.
- Grate the chocolate (optional) over everything and chill in the fridge overnight. Serve.

Nutrition-Per Serving: Calories: 231Kcal, Total Fat: 9g, Total Carbs: 31g, Protein: 8g

BLACK CHERRY CAKE

This is a perfect dessert for cake lovers. It is super easy to put together, requires very few ingredients, yet tastes like heaven.

| Prep time: 5 min | Cook time: 0 min | Servings: 4 |

Ingredients

- 5 oz butter
- 5 oz caster sugar
- 5 oz flour
- 4 eggs
- 5 oz chocolate, melt
- Black cherries

Instructions

- Preheat your oven to 350°F then butter and flour the cake tin.
- In a mixing bowl, combine cream butter, sugar, and flour until well mixed and fluffy.
- Separate the egg yolks and egg whites then beat the egg whites.
- Mix the egg yolk in the butter and flour mixture.
- Add the melted chocolate. Make sure it's not too warm so your eggs do not cook. Finally, gently stir in the egg whites to the mixture – do not overmix as the egg whites bring fluffiness to the cake.
- Spread the batter in the cake tin and sprinkle the top with black cherries.
- Bake for 45minutes then leave to cool before serving. Enjoy.

Nutrition-Per Serving: Calories: 307Kcal, Total Fat: 17g, Total Carbs: 33g, Protein: 5g

PRSPAJLE (FRIED PASTRY)

These delectable pastries will satisfy the taste buds of you and your family. They are made with only a few ingredients but taste delicious.

| Prep time: 15 min | Cook time: 15 min | Servings: 12 |

Ingredients

- ½ tbsp dried yeast
- ½ cup sugar
- 1 ½ cup flour
- 1 egg
- ½ cup warm milk
- Vegetable oil for frying

Instructions

- Place yeast in ⅓ cup warm water and 1 tbsp sugar. Stir until well combined. Place the mixture in a warm place until it bubbles.
- Add flour, 1 tbsp sugar, and a pinch of salt in a mixing bowl. Mix until well combined.
- In another mixing bowl, beat the egg with milk then add the mixture to the flour.
- Add the yeast mixture and mixture until a smooth dough is formed. Knead the dough on a floured surface until smooth and elastic. Transfer the dough to a greased bowl and cover with a towel. Let it rise until doubled in size.
- Divide the dough into 12 portions and roll out each portion into 3 inches rounds.
- Heat oil in a saucepan and deep fry the rounds while turning them halfway through the cooking session.
- Remove the pastries and dry them on paper towels. Dust with sugar and serve.

Nutrition-Per Serving: Calories: 320Kcal, Total Fat: 20g, Total Carbs: 26g, Protein: 7g

PLUM JAM BISCUITS

These are scrumptious melt-in-your-mouth biscuits that everyone will enjoy. The plum jam, which helps keep the jam in biscuits instead of leaking out when cooking, is the genius behind their perfection.

| Prep time: 20 min | Cook time: 15 min | Servings: 24 |

Ingredients

- *2 sticks butter, softened*
- *1 ¼ cup cream*
- *2 tbsp vanilla sugar*
- *1 ½ tbsp baking powder*
- *2 2/3 cups plain flour*
- *24 tbsp plum jam*
- *½ cup caster sugar*

Instructions

- In a mixing bowl, mix butter, cream, sugar, and baking powder until well combined.
- Add flour slowly while mixing until you achieve soft and stretchy dough. Knead for 5 minutes.
- Roll the dough out on a working surface then use a pizza cutter to cut out 6-inch triangles.
- Place the triangle with the wide side facing you then add a tbsp of the plum jam. Roll the triangle over the jam to form u shape.
- Repeat the process with the rest of the triangles. Bake the biscuits at 395°F until the biscuits are golden brown.
- Roll in caster sugar and serve.

Nutrition-Per Serving: Calories: 146Kcal, Total Fat: 9g, Total Carbs: 17g, Protein: 2g

BLACKBERRY PIE

Most Croatian families enjoy this blackberry pie. It's flavorful, with a buttery crust and an incredibly juicy blackberry filling.

| Prep time: 40 min | Cook time: 50 min | Servings: 6 |

Ingredients

- 1 ⅓ cups flour
- ¾ tbsp baking powder
- 1 ½ sticks butter, chopped
- 1 cup caster sugar
- 2 eggs

- *3 ½ cups berries*
- *1 tbsp vanilla extract*
- *1 tbsp lemon zest*
- *Icing sugar for garnish*

Instructions

- In your food processor, add flour, baking powder, butter, and half of the sugar. Pulse until the mixture resembles breadcrumbs.
- Add 2 egg yolks and continue to process until the mixture is a ball but soft.
- Transfer the ball to a floured working surface and cut ⅓ of the dough. Shape it into a disc, cover with a wrap and reserve it in the fridge for up to 30 minutes.
- Using your damp hands, press the rest of the dough on a greased pie dish then place it in the fridge to chill.
- Preheat your oven to 350F. Meanwhile, make the filling by whisking egg whites with a hand mixer until soft peak forms.
- Add the remaining sugar gradually while whisking until it's glossy.
- Fold in the berries, vanilla, and lemon zest until well combined. Scoop the mixture to the shell then cut the reserved dough into slices to make a cover.
- Bake for 50 minutes or until a knife inserted at the center comes out clean and is golden brown. Dust with icing sugar and serve.

Per Serving: Calories: 505Kcal, Total Fat: 25g, Total Carbs: 66g, Protein: 5g

COFFEE CRÈME CARAMEL

This coffee crème caramel is rich and flavorful. Its beauty and creaminess are due to baking it in a water bath. Even better, you may use decaffeinated coffee and still get the same delight from this treat.

| Prep time: 5 min | Cook time: 0 min | Servings: 4 |

Ingredients

Caramel

- 2 cups sugar

Coffee Crème

- 2 cups milk
- 1 tbsp coffee powder
- 4 eggs
- ⅓ cup sugar
- 1 tbsp vanilla extract

Instructions

Caramel

- Pour the sugar in a saucepan and heat over medium heat until it starts to melt. Start to shake the saucepan until all sugar has melted and is dark in color.
- Pour it into dishes and tip it round such that it covers the base and the sides.

Coffee Crème

- Preheat your oven to 270°F.
- Add milk and coffee to another saucepan. Whisk gently and let the mixture heat.
- Meanwhile, whisk together eggs, sugar, and vanilla extract in a mixing bowl. Pour the mixture into the hot milk and mix until well combined.
- Pour the mixture through a sieve into a measuring cup then pour the sieved mixture into the caramel-lined dishes.
- Place the dishes in a baking pan and place them in the oven.
- Pour boiled water in the baking pan to surround the dish up to ⅔ in depth. Bake for 25 minutes.
- Let it rest to cool. Cover with cling wrap and transfer it to the fridge.
- Loosen the sides with a palette knife and invert on a plate. Serve and enjoy!

Nutrition-Per Serving: Calories: 254Kcal, Total Fat: 14g, Total Carbs: 66g, Protein: 12g

Printed in Great Britain
by Amazon